Dyscalculi Matters

Effective ways of working with children who struggle with maths

Book 2 Ages 7-9

Frances Adlam

essential resources

Title:	Dyscalculia Matters Effective ways of working with children who struggle with maths – Book 2: Ages 7–9
Author:	Frances Adlam
Designer:	Red Sea Books
Editor:	Tanya Tremewan
Book code:	0710
ISBN:	978-1-927190-84-5
Published:	2012
Publisher:	Essential Resources Educational Publishers Limited

United Kingdom:	Australia:	New Zealand:
Units 8–10 Parkside	PO Box 906	PO Box 5036
Shortgate Lane	Strawberry Hills	Invercargill
Laughton, BN8 6DG	NSW 2012	
ph: 0845 3636 147	ph: 1800 005 068	ph: 0800 087 376
fax: 0845 3636 148	fax: 1800 981 213	fax: 0800 937 825

Websites: www.essentialresources.com.au
www.essentialresources.co.nz

Copyright: Text: © Frances Adlam, 2012
Edition and illustrations: © Essential Resources Educational Publishers Limited, 2012

About the author: Frances Adlam, a highly experienced and creative educator and therapist, has 20 years of teaching experience, is considered a "gifted teacher" by many, and over the last 15 years has been involved in teaching the arts, creativity, multiple intelligences and working with creatively gifted children. She has lectured in New Zealand and been an adviser for teachers in the aforementioned areas. She is also a published children's author, a dancer and a playwright. She currently works as an educator and therapist for children in her private practice, Out of the Box, where she specialises in working with children who are on the spectra of dyslexia, ADHD, Asperger's syndrome and autism. Frances has written many resources for Essential Resources, some of which are under her former name, Frances Reed. You can find out more about Frances at www.outofthebox.net.nz

Copyright notice:

Schools and teachers who buy this book have permission to reproduce it within their present school by photocopying, or if in digital format, by printing as well. Quantities should be reasonable for educational purposes in that school and may not be used for non-educational purposes nor supplied to anyone else. Copies made from this book, whether by photocopying or printing from a digital file, are to be included in the sampling surveys of Copyright Licensing Limited (New Zealand), Copyright Agency Limited (Australia) or Copyright Licensing Agency (United Kingdom).

For further information on your copyright obligations, visit: New Zealand: www.copyright.co.nz, Australia: www.copyright.com.au, United Kingdom: www.cla.co.uk

Contents

Introduction	4
How can we assess for dyscalculia?	4
How do the key maths skills relate to dyscalculia?	4
Anxiety and dyscalculia	5
Best practice for teaching children with dyscalculia	6
An overview of the series	6
A box of resources	7
Hundred square	8
Activities	9
Pre-maths skills	9
1–100 (4)	10
Happy families	14
Partitioning for easy numbers	15
Splitting and partitioning	16
Adding with partitioning	17
It's a problem	18
Subtracting (4)	19
Adding with partitioning and re-grouping (2)	23
Make me a sum	25
Bundle me up	26
Fractions (3)	27
Adding fractions	30
Introducing decimals	31
Shopping with money	32
Decimal charts	33
Adding and subtracting decimals	34
Subtracting using equal addition	35
Groups of tables	36
Sharing groups of tables	37
Times tables	38
Thinking about times tables for children with dyscalculia	38
2 times table	39
Dividing with the 2 times table	40
3 times table	41
Dividing with the 3 times table	42
4 times table	43
Dividing with the 4 times table	44
5 times table	45
Dividing with the 5 times table	46
General times table games	47
Maths activities	48
Assessment	50
Assessment for general maths knowledge and strategies	50
Assessment for dyscalculia and maths difficulties	51
Index of maths concepts	55

Introduction

Dyscalculia Matters? Yes it does! Dyscalculia is an umbrella term used for a learning difficulty with maths. It is often thought of as the maths equivalent of dyslexia. The Department for Education and Skills in the UK describes dyscalculia in this way:

> Developmental dyscalculia is a condition that affects the ability to acquire arithmetical skills. Dyscalculia learners may have difficulty understanding simple number concepts, lack an intuitive grasp of numbers, and have problems learning number facts and procedures. Even if they produce a correct answer or use a correct method, they may do so mechanically and without confidence.[1]

This series recognises that dyscalculia *does* matter. It offers a maths programme through to age 9 that can help students with dyscalculia because it is grounded in an understanding of their needs and best teaching practice with this group of children in particular.

How can we assess for dyscalculia?

It is very difficult for teachers to specifically assess a child for dyscalculia. One reason is that research and assessment procedures to do with dyscalculia are far less common than they are for dyslexia. In addition, the long- and short-term style of memory skills required for maths are the same memory skills required for language – so a child with dyslexia who has weak memory skills will also find maths difficult in areas where memory is required. For example, children with weak working memory skills may find speed tests very difficult indeed. So like many learning difficulties, dyscalculia overlaps with other learning conditions.

What we do know, however, is that if a child is struggling to progress in maths at a rate that we expect, the only way to move that child forward is to teach number concepts: explicitly, sequentially, with small steps and in a multi-sensory way. The number concepts are set out in such a way in this series.

How do the key maths skills relate to dyscalculia?

The following are three key skills that anyone needs to be successful in maths – and that children with dyscalculia struggle with.

1. **A sense of number** (also called a sense of numerosity): In language, children need to know that words are made up of sounds and then that those sounds can be represented by letters. Similarly in maths they need to grasp that number is all around us. They need a sense that if I have 5 blocks, that is more than 2 blocks. Then they need to understand that the idea of number is represented by symbols we call numerals.

   The child with dyscalculia does not have a sense of number. They cannot grasp that the numeral 9 represents a quantity of nine things. As this concept of number cannot be grasped, it is difficult (if not impossible) to compare numbers, order numbers and make estimations about numbers.

---

[1] Department for Education and Skills (2001) *The National Numeracy Strategy Guidance to Support Pupils with Dyslexia and Dyscalculia*. London: DfES.

As maths is a highly linear subject, in that all number facts build logically from the previous number facts, if the child cannot grasp the sense of number they can never make logical deductions of the following fact. For example, if I cannot get a real sense of why 2 + 2 = 4, I will not be able to make the link that 2 + 3 must therefore equal 5.

2. **An ability to sequence and order numerical facts.** Maths relies on patterns, sequences and order. If I can sequence even numbers into an ascending pattern, I can also sequence them into a descending pattern. If I understand that every other number is an even number, I can deduce that, starting from a different number, every other number will be an odd number. I can move forward to see the relationship between 2 + 2 = 4 and 4 + 4 = 8 so 2 + 2 + 2 + 2 must also equal 8.

The child with dyscalculia finds it difficult to sequence numbers. They do not intuitively grasp sequences and patterns. This means it is extremely difficult for them to use strategies or logical shortcuts when calculating. They need to start all maths problems from scratch, making maths a very slow process.

3. **Short-term memory, long-term memory and working memory.** Learners need short-term memory to remember the sum that is being asked and if it connects to the previous one (ie, forms a pattern). They need long-term memory to remember maths facts. As soon as the working memory and short-term memory have processed a concept, the maths facts need to be stored in the long-term memory so that the other two memory processes can focus on learning the next concept. Typically learners can retrieve facts from the long-term memory when needed to apply them to a strategy for solving a problem. The working memory allows them to make connections between stored facts and new instructions.

The child with dyscalculia usually has all three types of memory working in a weak way. The short-term memory easily forgets what the task is. The long-term memory cannot retain facts, and those that it does retain are very difficult to retrieve. The working memory cannot make connections between facts that cannot be stored or retrieved. For a child with dyscalculia, it can seem like they always have to start the whole maths process from the beginning.

Anxiety and dyscalculia

Maths is a linear subject in that progress is made by learning concepts and then transferring those concepts as facts in the long-term memory. As the learner works through levels of maths, they gain more and more facts for the memory to hold onto – facts that they need to be able to retrieve easily so that they can apply them automatically to solve the next layer of problems.

As the overview of the key skills above identifies, the child with dyscalculia does not have such a memory so finds it very difficult to retrieve and apply these facts. When faced with solving a problem using previously learnt facts, their mind draws a blank. This experience can be extremely frustrating, upsetting and demoralising. It can lead to anxiety over maths and sometimes behavioural problems.

Introduction

Teachers need to be sensitive to such anxiety as it can have long-lasting effects. The key strategies are to constantly observe the underlying issues for the child in any given problem, be creative in teaching the problem and use multi-sensory teaching and learning methods. There is nothing more wonderful for a teacher than when a child who struggles with maths suddenly "gets it".

Best practice for teaching children with dyscalculia

At the heart of dyscalculia is a lack of number sense and poor memory. For this reason, hands-on resources are imperative. Common mathematical resources are wonderful – blocks, Cuisenaire rods, counters, number lines and so on – but also think out of the box: glass stones, little animals, stickers, chocolates, buttons and shells all work a treat.

Best practice must include:
- multi-sensory ideas – for example, get children walking out their numbers, jumping onto even numbers, playing the drum as they count
- explicit teaching of a concept – get children to tell you what they have learnt at the end of the lesson and *during* the lesson
- sequential teaching of concepts
- lots of practice and revision of a concept
- insight into *how* the child views the maths concept.

An overview of the series

The first book in the *Dyscalculia Matters* series is aimed at ages 5–7; the second book is aimed at ages 7–9. However, the boundaries are not fixed. For example, Book 1 would also work well with initial teaching of children who are new to school and sets out first concepts that would be useful for older children to return to if they are struggling with a higher level of maths.

Important features of this series

The maths programme set out in this series can be followed sequentially for children with dyscalculia or individual activities can be chosen to complement an existing programme. The activities are written for the *teacher* to prepare. All lessons will need hands-on materials to start with (and possibly for longer). Worksheets have been avoided deliberately as they are an ineffective way of learning for children with dyscalculia, or with general maths difficulties.

Slow and steady

Teachers are inundated with curriculum areas, assessments and learning goals they have to cover in a set amount of time. This approach to teaching and learning will not work with children who have dyscalculia. Children with dyscalculia will require:
- lots of repetition
- a teacher who listens to where they have a block with their number sense and who creatively unpacks that block for them
- lots of revisiting of previous knowledge and strategies
- lots of *slow* and *steady* teaching.

A box of resources

For children who struggle with maths, it is best to have a separate box of inspiring objects that can be counted, sorted, shared, added and mathematically explored – as these children will need to use resources for much longer than their same-age peers. Also, little toy animals can be easier for a child to relate to than "faceless" counters and can intrigue a child, drawing them in to the maths concept being taught.

It is usually best to organise and label the toys in groups of 10 – or whatever concept is being taught (unless sorting *is* the concept being taught). With this advance organisation, you can start teaching immediately without having to wait for children to find 10 animals. Once children get more organised with their maths, they can quickly organise all the objects into groups of 10 for you at the end of the lesson.

The following are some ideas for your box. You do not need to have them all at once. You may just want some of the objects, or you may collect objects over time. Let your own creative, playful and mathematical juices free too in assembling your box.

Some ideas for your box of resources

- Blocks that click into each other for building towers – at least five different colours
- Ten rods; one blocks bagged up into tens
- Boxes for putting objects in
- Cloth for placing objects neatly on so they don't get lost on the desk
- Magnetic numbers
- Magnetic fractions
- 20 copies of faces, laminated
- Large number line (big enough to walk on)
- Copy of a hundred square (see the next page; laminate it for durable use)
- 20 animals that are all the same – such as all fish, all spiders or all bats
- Balls for bouncing on numbers that are called out
- Bean bags for numbers that are called out
- Tubs of 100 small animals, 100 stones etc
- Play money
- Three-dimensional and two-dimensional shapes

© Essential Resources Educational Publishers Ltd, 2012

A box of resources

Hundred square

1	2	3	4	5	6	7	8	9	10
11	12	13	14	15	16	17	18	19	20
21	22	23	24	25	26	27	28	29	30
31	32	33	34	35	36	37	38	39	40
41	42	43	44	45	46	47	48	49	50
51	52	53	54	55	56	57	58	59	60
61	62	63	64	65	66	67	68	69	70
71	72	73	74	75	76	77	78	79	80
81	82	83	84	85	86	87	88	89	90
91	92	93	94	95	96	97	98	99	100

© Essential Resources Educational Publishers Ltd, 2012

Activities

Pre-maths skills

It is extremely important that older children at primary school are made to feel positive about using resources. You can encourage this attitude by using resources to explain a concept to the *whole* class rather than differentiating between those who use resources and those who do not.

Explore

- Give the children blocks of 1 000, 100 and 10. Ask them to use the blocks to work out how to make different numbers, such as 1 420 and 2 350.

- Ask the children to explain, tell or show how we know that the 1 000-block is 10 lots of 100. Do the same for the 100-block (ie, how we know it is 10 lots of 10).

- Ask the children to sort and organise sets of money: the coins worth $1, $2, 50 cents etc. How many different ways can $1 be made with the cents?

- Facilitate a discussion in which the children discuss what they could buy for $5 from different types of shops: the dairy, the hardware store, the book shop, the butcher etc.

- Ask the children to feel and explore three-dimensional shapes. How does this shape sit? Is the bottom a triangle or a square? What difference does that make to the overall shape?

- Ask the children to set out magnetic fractions. Which fractions can be exchanged evenly (1/5 for 2/10 etc)? What do we notice?

- Ask the children to set out their 3 times table in blocks: 1 tower of 3, 2 towers of 3 etc.

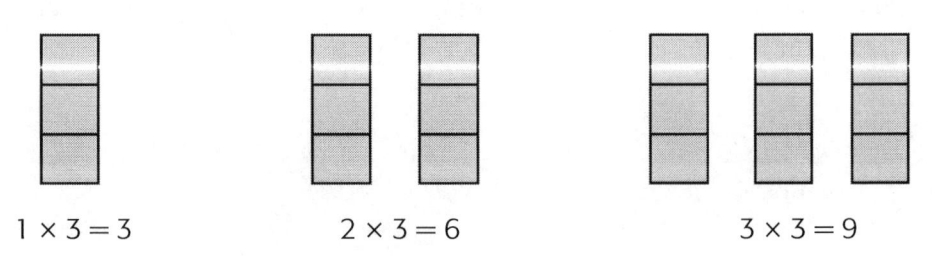

    1 × 3 = 3   2 × 3 = 6   3 × 3 = 9

© Essential Resources Educational Publishers Ltd, 2012

Activities

Instantly recognising 1–100

Resources

- Numbers from 1–100 on separate laminated cards
- Masking tape

Explore

Give one child the numbers 1–10 and another child the numbers 11–20 to place around the room with masking tape. Ask the other children to look for numbers that you call out – 15, 12, 18 etc. Who can find them first?

Instructions (teacher to students)

1. (Ask another child to place the numbers 21–30 around the room so that numbers 1–30 are now displayed. Give each child five numbers to find quickly. With a small group, you could whisper the numbers or provide them on pieces of paper. With a large group, children can work in pairs and give each other numbers to look for.)

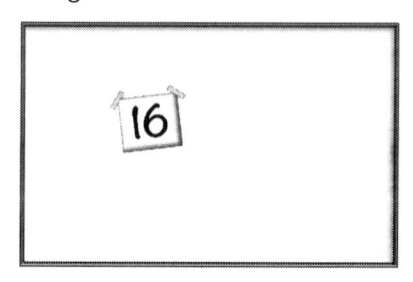

2. Who has found the number 16? Point to where it is. Who has found the number 12? Point to where it is. We are going to work *fast*.

3. We will move outside for space. I am going to give you, as a group, the numbers from 1–100, except for five of the numbers which I am keeping. You need to tell me in less than 2 minutes which numbers I have. I also want you to tell me how you worked the answer out.

4. Do you think the strategy you used for finding out the answer was the most efficient one you could have used? Did anyone have some other ideas?

5. This time I am giving you the numbers 1–100, except for 12 numbers which I am keeping. I want you to tell me which 12 numbers I have in 1 minute.

6. Now I want you to place all the numbers 1–100 in a hundred square on the ground. I want all the tens in a vertical line: 10, 20, 30, 40 etc. See how long this takes you.

7. I am going to show you the number *after*. Here is 45; now this is the number after. Here is 78; now this is the number *after*. Tell me which direction I go to find the number after.

8. (Repeat step 7 but show the number *before*.)

Explain

I need you to explain to your partner what *after* means and what *before* means in relation to the hundred square. I am going to choose one pair to share their explanations with us all.

Activities

Instantly recognising 1–100 and more

Resources (per child)

- A laminated hundred square (enlarge the copy on page 8 to about 20 cm by 20 cm)
- Whiteboard marker

Explore

Give each child a laminated hundred square. Call out some numbers (within patterns) for each child to circle with a marker; for example: 70, 71, 72, 73, 74, 75, 76, 77, 78, 79, 80. Ask each child what they notice about 70 and 71 (70 is on a different line, which can confuse some children). Follow up with questions such as, "If all the 70s are in one line, where do you think the 60s will be?"

Instructions (teacher to students)

1. Find the line with the numbers in their 80s as quickly as possible. Find the line with the numbers in their 30s as quickly as possible, and now 50s. Do your eyes immediately know in which direction to look, or are they searching all over the hundred square?
2. What do you notice if you find the number 9 and then look down that row? (Every number ends in a 9.)
3. What do you notice if we circle all the even numbers?
4. What do you notice if we circle all the odd numbers?
5. Let's circle all the odd numbers starting from 57. (Repeat, starting from 69.)
6. How many do we need to add to get from 87 to 97?
7. How many do we need to add to get from 56 to 66? (Check that each child is clear and confident that when they are adding from 56 to 66, the number 57 is where the counting starts.)
8. How many do we need to add to get from 56 to 76?
9. How many do we need to subtract to get from 64 to 54?
10. (Repeat the step 9 process for subtracting from 34 to 24, and from 20 to 10.)

Next steps

If the children are ready, extend them with questions such as:

- How many do we need to add to get from 34 to 47?
- How do we count this?
- What is the most effective way of counting this?

Explain

Explain to your partner how to quickly add up, and subtract, in tens on the hundred square.

© Essential Resources Educational Publishers Ltd, 2012

Activities

1–100 off we go

Resources (per child)
- A laminated hundred square (see page 8)
- Whiteboard marker

Explore

Ask each child to choose a pattern on the hundred square they would like to explore and to identify it with the whiteboard marker. Children can share the pattern they have found.

Instructions (teacher to students)

1. Find the number 30. How many numbers do we count until we get to 40?
2. Find the number 35. How many numbers do we have to count until we get to 40?
3. Find the number 77. How many numbers do we have to count until we get to 80?
4. Find the number 28. How many numbers do we have to count until we get to 30?
5. What pattern do you notice between our addition facts to 10 and adding numbers in the hundred square?

$$7 + 3 = 10 \qquad 8 + 2 = 10$$
$$77 + 3 = 80 \qquad 28 + 2 = 30$$

6. Let's practise the pattern (in steps 3–5 above) and see if it helps us add our numbers with speed.
7. (Point to 56.) How many do I need to get to 60 (quickly)?
8. (Point to 67.) How many do I need to get to 70 (quickly)?
9. (Point to 78.) How many do I need to get to 80 (quickly)?

Next steps

- If I place a sum like this on the board: 78 + ? = 80, can we do this without looking at the hundred square?
- If I place a sum like this on the board: 46 − ? = 40, can we do this without looking at the hundred square? (If so, give lots more questions like this.)

Explain

I need you to explain to your partner how we can quickly know that if I have 77, I will add 3 to get to 80.

Activities

1–100 mini patterns

Resources (per child)

- A laminated hundred square (see page 8)
- Whiteboard marker

Explore

Ask each child to choose a pattern on the hundred square that they have not chosen before and they would like to explore. They identify it with the whiteboard marker. Children can share the pattern they have found.

Instructions (teacher to students)

1. We can notice that if we have 36 + ? = 40, we add the *next* 4 numbers – 37, 38, 39, 40. That is, when we are adding we start on the *next* number. We can notice that if we have 36 – ? = 30, we take away the 5 numbers *before* – 35, 34, 33, 32, 31, and we take away the number 36 itself as well. That is, the way we count on the hundred square when we are adding is different from the way we count when we are subtracting. (Which number to start on can be extremely confusing for children with dyscalculia so this point may need lots of work.)

36 – ? = 30

21	22	23	24	25	26	27	28	29	30
31	32	33	34	35	(36)	37	38	39	40

36 + ? = 40

2. We can notice: 36 + 4 = 40; 36 – 6 = 30.
3. I will write some sums on the board. Answer them using the hundred square.

```
47 – 7 =        98 – 8 =
35 – 5 =        76 – 6 =
24 – 4 =        29 – 9 =
14 – 4 =        41 – 1 =
```

Explain

I need you to explain to your partner how we can quickly know that if I have 35 – 5, the answer will be 30. Show your partner on the hundred square which number you start counting from.

© Essential Resources Educational Publishers Ltd, 2012

Activities

Happy families

Resources (per child)

- A laminated hundred square (see page 8)
- 4 lots of ten arrays, each with removable circles

Explore

Ask each child to create patterns by adding circles to the array and subtracting others from it.

Instructions (teacher to students)

1. Place all the circles in the ten arrays. We have 40 altogether. How many will we have if we take 5 away? We can write this as: 40 − 5 = 35. So now we have 35. If we add 5, how many will we have? We can write this as: 35 + 5 = 40.

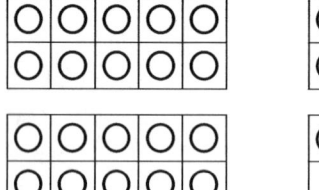

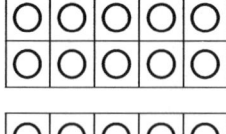

2. What pattern can you see with: 40 − 5 = 35 and 35 + 5 = 40?

3. Place all the circles in the ten arrays. We have 40 altogether. How many will we have if we take 6 away? We can write this as: 40 − 6 = 34. Now we have 34. If we add 6, how many will we have? We can write this as: 34 + 6 = 40.

4. (Repeat the process in steps 2 and 3 as many times as required.)

5. See if you can fill in the following:

   40 − 8 = 32
   32 + ? = 40
   40 − 11 = 29
   29 + ? = 40

   Let's see if we can see the family of patterns this way round:

   33 + 7 = 40
   40 − ? = 33

6. Using your array tell me the different ways you worked out the answers (in step 5).

Explain

Explain to your partner why the sums involved in adding and subtracting with the same set of numbers are called a *family of facts*.

Activities

Partitioning for easy numbers

Resources (per child)
- 2 ten rods
- 20 one blocks

Explore
Ask each child to sort and explore their rods and blocks.

Instructions (teacher to students)

1. Make the number 17 with a ten rod and 7 one blocks. Place the one blocks next to the ten rod. We are now going to do this sum: 17 + 8 = ___
   - Step 1: Get eight ones. We are going to split these up to make them easier to work with. How many ones do we need to take the number 17 up to 20? (3)
   - Step 2: We have split 8 up into 3 and … how many are left? (5) So we have split 8 up into 3 and 5. We have done this because it is easier to add with 20 than to add with 17.
   - Step 3: Now we have 20 (17 + 3) + 5 = ___

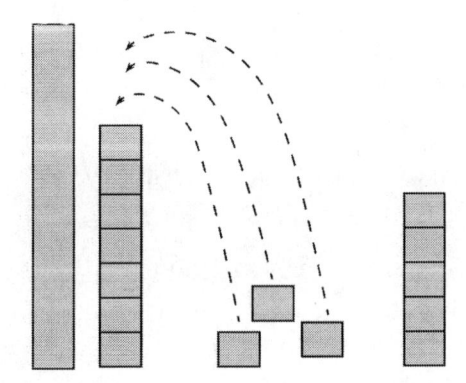

   Who can tell me the answer and the three steps we use to get there?

2. We are now going to do these sums with the three steps:

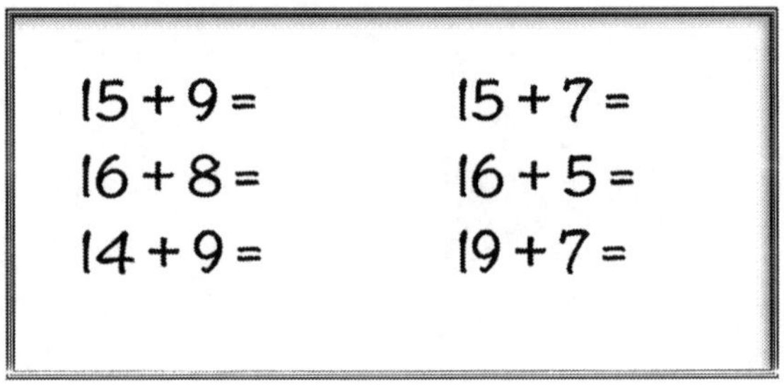

   15 + 9 =   15 + 7 =
   16 + 8 =   16 + 5 =
   14 + 9 =   19 + 7 =

Explain
How many ways can we split these numbers: 7, 8, 9? Explain our findings to a partner.

Activities

Splitting and partitioning

Resources

- Photos of different partitions for buildings and rooms
- 2 ten rods per child
- 20 one blocks per child

Explore

Ask each child to look at the photos of partitions. Discuss what they think a partition does and how it works. What is its purpose?

Instructions (teacher to students)

1. We are going to split our blocks and numbers. Write this number: 9. With your one blocks, see how many ways you can partition or split up 9: 4–5, 3–6, 2–7, 1–8.

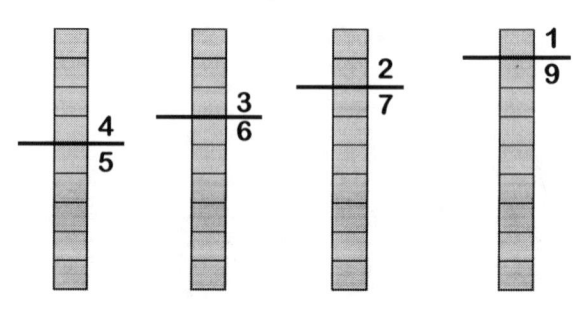

2. Let's write the number 8. How many ways can we split this number?

3. Let's write the number 7. How many ways can we split this number? Tell me any patterns you are noticing.

4. Now we are going to move onto numbers that contain a 10. Let's write this number: 16. Make the number 16 with a ten rod and six one blocks. Split this number into 10 and 6. Now split this number into 10, 3 and 3. What would we have to do to split up the 10? (Exchange the rod for 10 one blocks.) Can you split the number 16 up into 9 and 7? If we split it into 8 on one side, what number would be on the other side? When we place the *ten* on one side and the *ones* on another side, we call this *partitioning*.

5. (Repeat the process in step 4 until children are confidently noticing patterns.)

6. Let's put the 16 back together again (one ten rod and six ones). How can we see how many more we need to get to 20?

7. (Repeat step 6 with different numbers.)

Next step

Practise partitioning numbers with hundreds, tens and ones.

Explain

Explain to your partner how we partition numbers. Is there just one way to partition numbers? When else do we use the idea of partitioning?

Activities

Adding with partitioning

Resources (per child)
- 5 ten rods
- 20 one blocks
- Piece of A4 cloth
- Ruler

Explore

Ask each child to sort and explore their rods and blocks.

Instructions (teacher to students)

1. Place the ruler down the middle of the cloth. On one side of the ruler, place 2 ten rods. On the other side, place the number 17 in blocks. We are going to add these numbers: 20 + 17. We are going to partition the 17 into a 10 and 7. We are going to put the ten rod on the other side of the ruler and turn the 20 into 30. We have 30 on one side and 7 on the other side. Let's add them together.

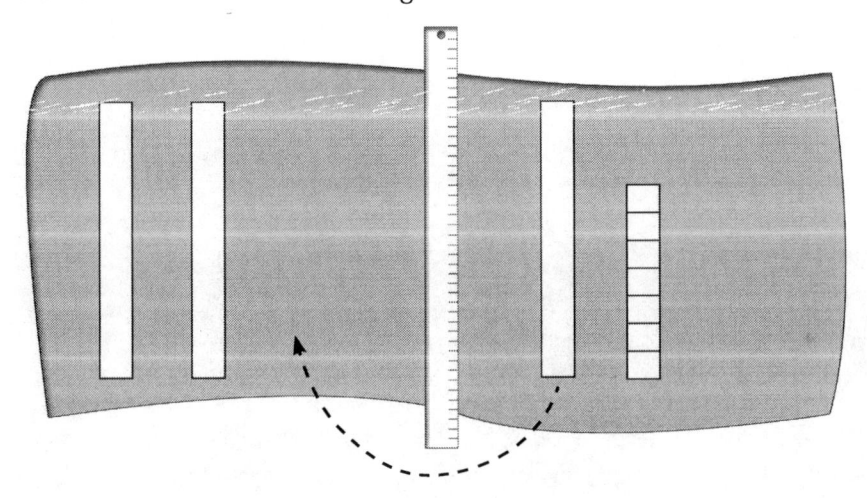

2. We are going to do the following sums by placing the numbers on the cloth first, on either side of the cloth. We are going to partition the ten by taking it to the other side of the cloth and then adding the ones. We will work with blocks on cloth first and then write the sum:

20 + 14 =	20 + 12 =
30 + 16 =	30 + 15 =
20 + 18 =	40 + 16 =
40 + 18 =	30 + 19 =

Explain

Explain to a partner how you partition the numbers into tens and ones. Share any patterns you notice when using this strategy.

Activities

It's a problem

Resources (per child)
- 5 ten rods
- 20 one blocks
- Piece of A4 cloth
- Ruler

Explore

Ask each child to sort and explore their rods and blocks.

Instructions (teacher to students)

1. Sometimes we have to solve a maths problem that is given in words. We need to think, what are we being asked to do? We will work on some word sums today and use the partitioning strategy to solve them.

2. This is an example of a problem: Joseph has 20 marbles. His friend, Martin, has 15 marbles. They decide to put their marbles together and work as a team. How many marbles do they have altogether?

   Here we are being asked: $20 + 15 =$ ___; or: $20 + 10 + 5 =$ ___

3. Try the following word sums. Use the partitioning strategy and write the sum down:
   - Ben has 30 game cards. His sister has 17 game cards. How many do they have altogether?
   - David has played a computer game 20 times. His brother has played the same computer game 18 times. How many times have the boys played the computer game altogether?
   - Ella has collected 20 bouncy balls. Her best friend, Molly, has collected 17 bouncy balls. How many do they have altogether?
   - Jasmine has 20 blue pens, 3 green pens and 5 black pens. Leo has 13 blue pens, 2 green pens and 2 purple pens. How many blue pens do they have between the two of them?
   - Frankie has 20 pet mice. Johnny has 14 pet mice. How many do they have altogether?

Explain

Tell a partner the different words that can be used to mean "add the two numbers".

Activities

Subtracting: Taking away an amount

Resources (per child)
- 10 one blocks
- Piece of A4 cloth
- Ruler
- Cup
- Number line 0–10

Explore

Ask each child to explore their blocks.

Instructions (teacher to students)

1. Place the 10 one blocks on one side of the ruler on the cloth. Make sure there are 10 – now we won't need to count them again. Take 1 away from the 10. How many do we have left? Place the 1 you have taken away under the cup. I could tell a story of subtraction. There were 10 nuts, 1 got eaten by a guinea pig – now there are 9.

2. We have 9 blocks left. Take 1 away from 9 and put it under the cup. How many do we have now? I can make up a story of subtraction. I had 9 lollies and my brother ate 1, so now there are 8.

3. (Repeat the process in steps 1–2, consistently taking one away until you get to 0.)

4. Now we will look at one sum and then work on it with the number line. Show me 10 one blocks. Take away 2 blocks by putting them under the cup. How many do we have left? Now get your number line. Where would we start this sum? (10) How would we show that we are taking 2 away on a number line? In which direction do we go? What do we count? (2 loops.) Where do we end up?

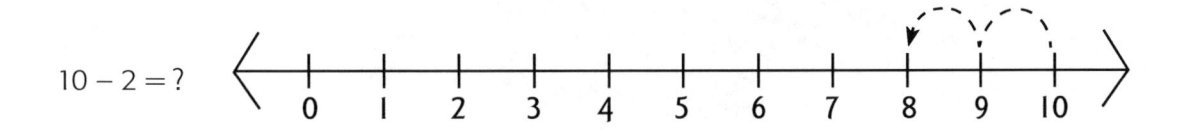

$10 - 2 = ?$

5. (Repeat the process in step 4 using a range of numbers between 1 and 10. Write the sum as an equation, eg, $10 - 7 = 3$, show it on the number line and write it as a story: I had 10 socks on the washing line, 3 flew away in the wind. How many do I have left?)

Explain

Explain to a partner how we show subtraction on a number line.

© Essential Resources Educational Publishers Ltd, 2012

Activities

Subtracting can give me two amounts

Resources (per child)
- 10 one blocks
- Piece of A4 cloth
- Ruler
- Cup
- Number line 0–10

Explore

Ask each child to explore their blocks.

Instructions (teacher to students)

1. Place the 10 one blocks on the cloth. Take away 2 blocks and put them under the cup. I now have 8 on the cloth and 2 under the cup. So I can say I have 2 amounts: by taking away 2 from 10, that gave me a 2 under the cup and an 8 on the cloth.

2. Now I have 8 on the cloth. Take away another 2. This time, place these 2 blocks on the table. I can say I have 6 on the cloth and 2 on the table. I can write the sum like this: 8 − 2 = 6. If I can see that I have 2 amounts, 2 and 6, I can see why addition is the opposite of subtracting, because 2 + 6 = 8.

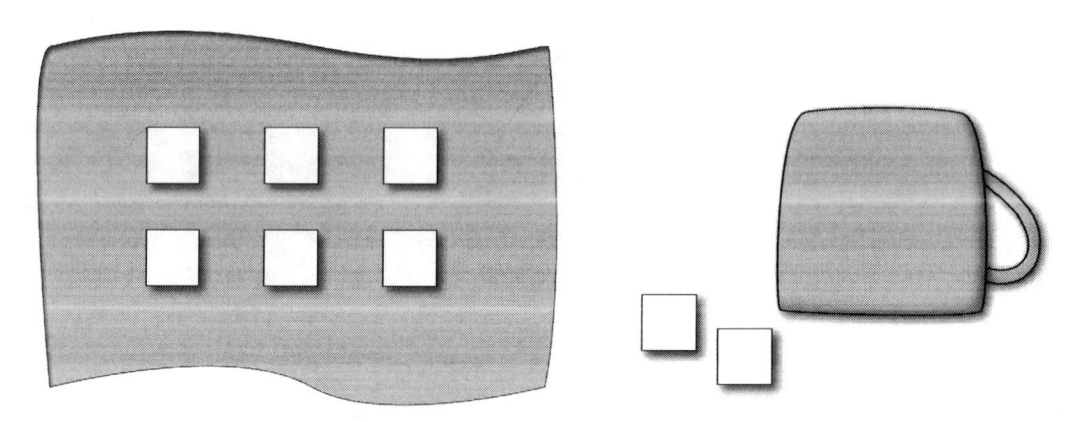

3. (Repeat the process in steps 1 and 2.)

4. Draw these sums, showing how when I subtract I can have 2 amounts:
    - 10 butterflies take away 4 butterflies as they fly north.
    - 10 frogs take away 5 frogs as they jump out of the pond.
    - 10 rats take away 6 rats as they run into town.
    - 10 cats take away 3 cats as they hide in the bush.

Explain

Explain to a partner how subtraction can be shown as having two amounts.

Activities

Subtracting can show difference

Resources

- Tape measure per pair
- Piece of A4 cloth per child
- 10 one blocks per child

Explore

Ask each child to explore their blocks.

Instructions (teacher to students)

1. I am going to ask two people to come up to the front. Can we see who is smaller and who is taller? We call the amount by which one is taller than the other the *difference*. Let's measure these two people next to a wall with a tape measure. Look, this child is 5 cm taller than this child. So the difference between them is 5 cm.

2. In pairs, find out what the difference is in your heights. Use a tape measure to work it out.

3. Now when we want to find the difference between two numbers, we can use subtraction. Look:

   7 marbles

   4 marbles

   To find the difference, I can say, "7 marbles subtract 4 marbles is 3 marbles. The difference is 3." It will look like this: 7 − 4 = 3.

4. See if you can use subtraction to find the difference between these pairs of marbles:
   - What is the difference between 7 marbles and 5 marbles?
   - What is the difference between 8 marbles and 4 marbles?
   - What is the difference between 9 marbles and 5 marbles?
   - What is the difference between 6 marbles and 3 marbles?

Explain

Explain to a partner why we can use subtraction to find out the difference between two numbers.

© Essential Resources Educational Publishers Ltd, 2012

Activities

Subtracting: Numbers get smaller

Resources (per child)

- 20 one blocks
- Piece of A4 cloth
- Ruler
- Cup
- Number line 0–20

Explore

Ask each child to explore their blocks.

Instructions (teacher to students)

1. Place the 20 blocks on one side of the ruler on the cloth. Make sure there are 20 – now we won't need to count them again. Take 1 away from the 20. How many do we have left? Place the 1 you have taken away under the cup. Let's just remember how many 10 – 1 is. What pattern can you see?

2. We have 19 blocks left. Take one away and put it under the cup. How many do we have left? Which is the bigger number: 19 or 18? So I can say that when I subtract, the number or amount left always gets smaller.

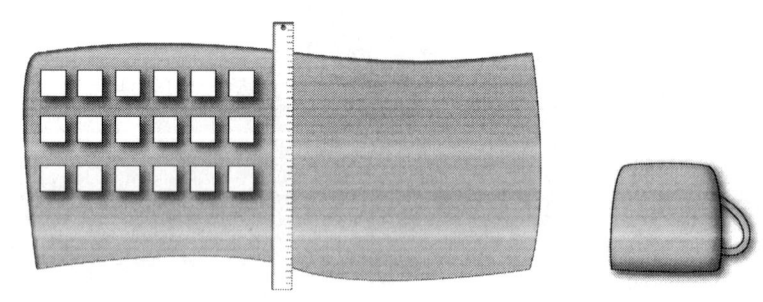

3. Let's think about this idea in real life:
    - If my family has 4 pizzas for dinner and we eat 3 of them, how many will we have left?
    - If my friends and I have 20 lollies and we eat 5 of them, how many will we have left?

4. We are going to change the name "take away" to *give away* for a moment. We are going to imagine we have a very kind character. What shall we call him? He is going to be a charitable person who gives things away. Let's create a story: Jack Give Away had 20 lunch snacks. He gave away 5 lunch snacks to some hungry friends. How many does he have left?

5. Make up some stories about Jack Give Away, using the numbers 1–20.

Explain

Explain to a partner how we can change *take away* to *give away*.

Activities

Adding with partitioning and re-grouping

Resources (per child)
- 10 ten rods
- 10 one blocks
- Cloth
- Ruler

Explore

Ask the children to make different groups and numbers with the ten rods and one blocks.

Instructions (teacher to students)

1. We are going to add: 43 + 9. Create 43 plus 9 with your rods and blocks. We are going to split up the 9 so that 7 blocks go over to the 43. Why do you think we have chosen the number 7? Because we now have 50 + 2. So the answer is 52.

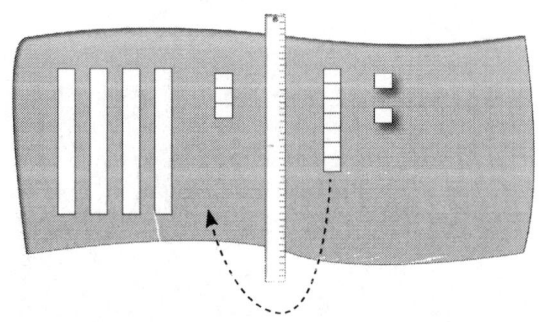

2. Let's do that again with this sum: 54 + 8. Create 54 plus 8 with your rods and blocks. We are going to split the 8 up so that 6 blocks go over to the 54. Why do you think we have chosen the number 6? Because we now have 60 + 2 = 62.

3. Now we are going to use the same strategy with these problems. We still work out a sum in each case; it just is a sum that has been written in words, like this:

   - The man has $56 in his bank account and $9 in his wallet. How much money does he have altogether? Show me how you would work this out using the rods and blocks and the partitioning strategy.

   - The children make $68 at their fundraising stall. The parents give them an extra $7 as a bonus. How much money do the children have altogether? Show me how you would work this out using the rods and blocks and the partitioning strategy.

   - There were 47 dogs in the dog home. Another 6 dogs come to join them. How many dogs are there now altogether? Show me how you would work this out using the rods and blocks and the partitioning strategy.

   - In East Street, 35 houses put their rubbish bins out before 8 o'clock on Wednesday morning. Another 9 houses put their rubbish out after 8 o'clock on Wednesday morning. How many houses have put out their rubbish altogether on this day?

Explain

Explain to a partner how to use the partitioning strategy. Show your partner using rods and blocks and one of the sums you have already completed.

© Essential Resources Educational Publishers Ltd, 2012

Activities

More please: Adding with partitioning and re-grouping

Resources (per child)

- 10 ten rods
- 10 one blocks

Explore

Ask the children to make different groups and numbers with the ten rods and one blocks.

Instructions (teacher to students)

Please complete the following problems, using the partitioning strategy:

1. Jenny has saved up $38. Her grandmother gives her another $8. How much money does she have altogether?

2. Ben had 27 Better Buy toy soldiers. His best friend gives him 7 more. How many does he have altogether?
3. Emma has 54 chocolate wrappers. Her best friend has 7. How many do they have altogether?
4. Bob had 46 nails in his box. He finds another 7 in his bag. How many nails does he have altogether?
5. James had 26 DVDs. For his birthday he gets another 6 DVDs as presents. How many DVDs does he have altogether?

Explain

Explain to a partner how to use the partitioning strategy. Show your partner using rods and blocks and one of the sums you have already completed.

Activities

Make me a sum

Resources (per child)

- 10 ten rods
- 10 one blocks
- Ball
- Paper and pen/pencil
- Sticking tack

Explore

Ask the children to make different groups and numbers with the ten rods and one blocks.

Instructions (teacher to students)

1. Show me the number 27 with the rods and blocks. How many ways can you split that? (20 + 7, 19 + 8 etc)

2. These numbers are going to be tacked to the wall: 38, 21, 45, 99, 57, 89, 13. Underneath are blank pieces of paper. On one piece of paper you will write your name. You will throw the ball at the number and see how many different sums you can come up with (orally first) for that number. When the whistle goes, you will write on your named piece of paper the sums you came up with. Then you will move on to another number. At the end of the game we will see who has the most sums.

38

Poppy
30 + 8 = 38
20 + 18 = 38

99

Isaac
90 + 9 = 99
80 + 19 = 99
70 + 29 = 99

3. Now we will alternate between addition sums and subtraction sums. For example, if the number you throw a ball at is 38, you need to come up with an *addition* sum to write on your piece of paper. Just do one sum, then move on to the next number. For this new number, when you throw the ball you need to come up with a *subtraction* sum that equals this answer. We will try to go as fast as we can around the numbers, giving just one sum (addition or subtraction) for each number.

4. Now we are going to take turns to call out the sums – so only one person will be calling out at any time. We will see how fast we can go.

Explain

Explain to a partner why there are many ways to create sums out of one number. It is of course to do with the way a number is split up – for addition. Choose one number and show your friend how you can get to that number/answer using addition and subtraction.

© Essential Resources Educational Publishers Ltd, 2012

Activities

Bundle me up

Resources (per child)

- 100 toothpicks and/or craft sticks and/or straws

Explore

Ask the children to count the resources, placing them in bundles of 10.

Instructions (teacher to students)

1. We are going to imagine that you are working in a shop. You have 100 sticks. Instead of counting them each time, what would be the most useful number to bundle them up in? (Discuss as required.)

2. Let's make sure everyone has bundled them up into tens. How many groups of 10 do you have?

3. Now they are bundled into groups of 10, what would be the easiest strategy to count 30 sticks?

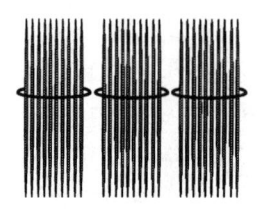

4. How could I count 40 sticks without starting all over again? (Hold the 30 in my head and add one more bundle.)

5. What strategy would be the quickest if a customer wanted only 8 sticks? (Take away 2 from a bundle.)

6. What strategy would be the quickest if a customer wanted 16 sticks? (Take away 4 from one bundle to leave 6 – and place those 6 with a 10 bundle.)

7. What strategy would be the quickest if a customer wanted 98 sticks? (Take away 2 sticks from one bundle and place the 8 left with all the other bundles.)

Explain

Explain to a partner why, if a customer needs 19 sticks, it is quicker to give them one complete bundle and another bundle with 1 taken out than it is to add 9 from the second bundle to the first bundle.

Activities

Fractions

Resources (per child)

- 10 bundles of 10 straws or sticks

Explore

Ask each child to count their bundles and add them up in different numbers of bundles quickly – 3 bundles plus 5 bundles?

Instructions (teacher to students)

1. You have 10 bundles of 10 sticks. You have 100 sticks altogether. Split your 10 bundles in half. Place the halves on the desk. How many bundles do you have on each side? (5 bundles or 50 sticks.)

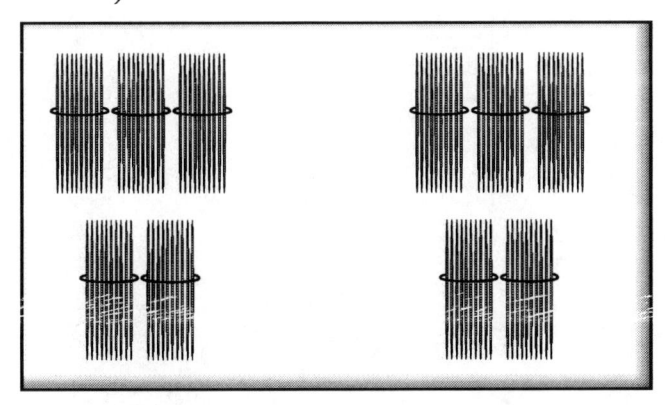

2. Take 2 bundles away. You are left with 8 bundles. Split these bundles in half and place them on the desk. How many bundles are on each side? (4 bundles, 40 sticks.)

3. Take 2 bundles away. You are left with 6 bundles. Split these bundles in half and place them on the desk. How many bundles on each side? (3 bundles, 30 sticks)

4. We can see half of 100 is 50 and half of 10 is 5. We can see half of 80 is 40 and half of 8 is 4. We can see half of 60 is 30 and half of 6 is 3. Explain to a partner what pattern you can see.

5. Fill in this chart.

Number	Half of number	Number	Half of number
100		10	
80		8	
60			3
40			2

Explain

Explain to a partner the strategy you used to fill in the chart.

© Essential Resources Educational Publishers Ltd, 2012

Activities

Fractions: Wholes and halves

Resources

- Pictures that commonly use halves

Explore

Ask each child look at the pictures below, and find some more, that show the use of halving.

Instructions (teacher to students)

Sort the pictures into groups of your choice and discuss with a partner why and when we may use the term *half*. Look at how half is written as a fraction: $\frac{1}{2}$. The 2 at the bottom of the fraction states that the *whole* has been split into 2 parts.

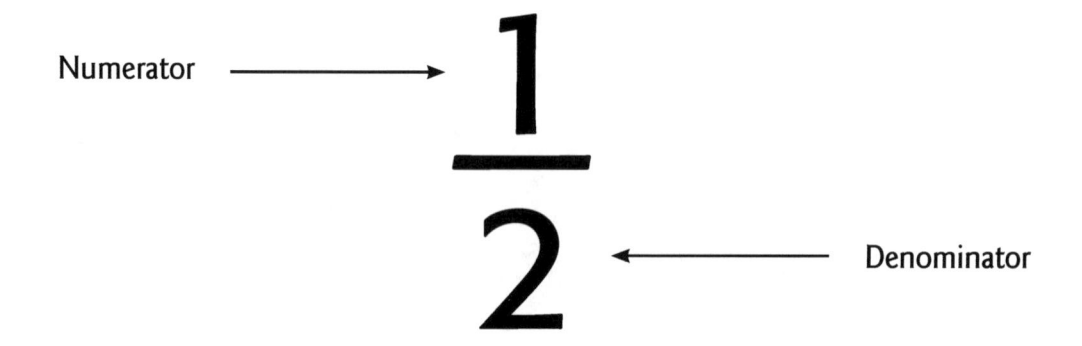

Numerator ⟶ $\frac{1}{2}$ ⟵ Denominator

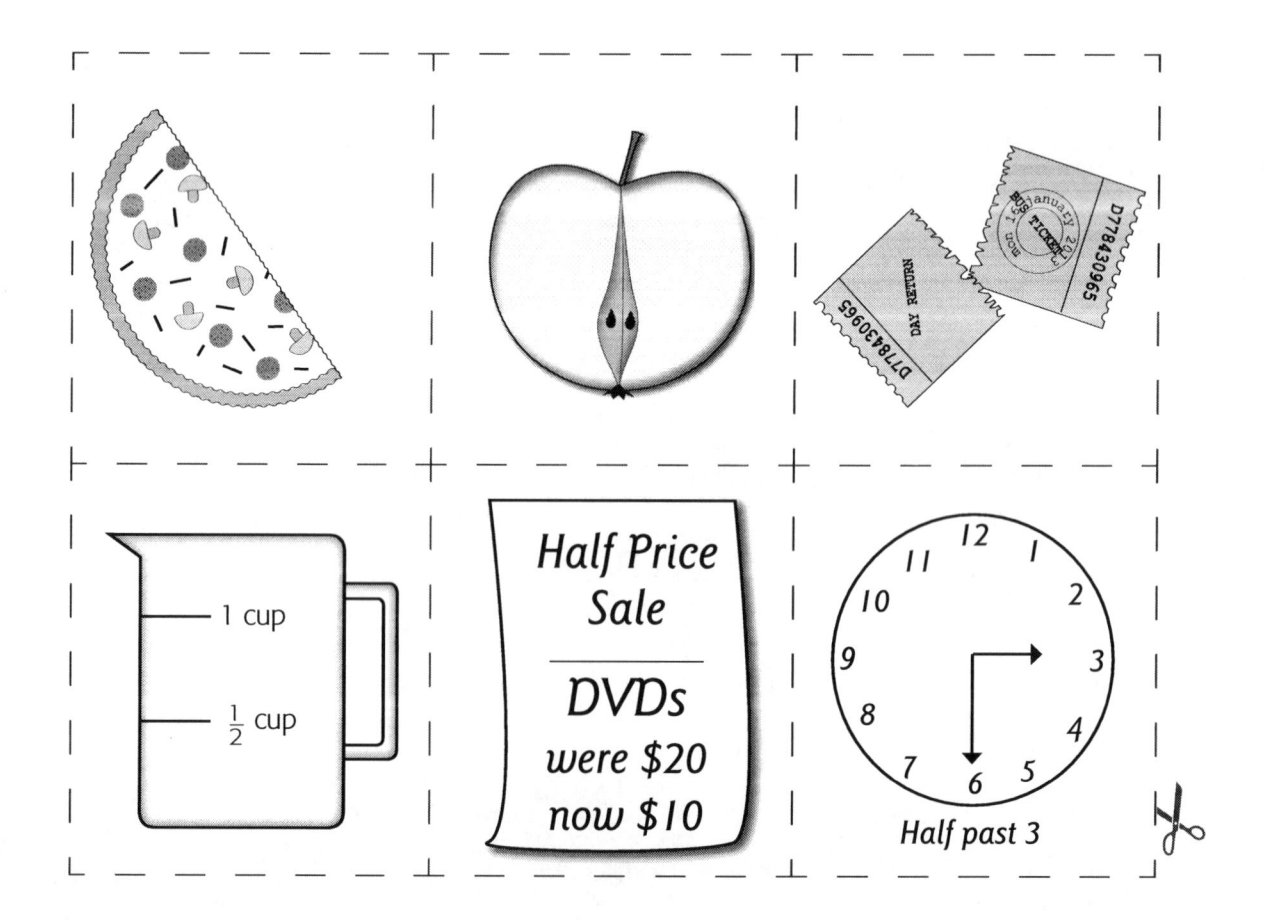

Half Price Sale
—
DVDs were $20 now $10

Half past 3

28 © Essential Resources Educational Publishers Ltd, 2012

Activities

Fractions: Wholes, halves, thirds and quarters

Resources (per child)
- 4 slices of bread or 4 cup cakes or 4 chocolate bars
- Plastic knife (or another safe alternative)
- Cards showing fractions in numerical form: 1, $\frac{1}{2}$, $\frac{1}{3}$, $\frac{1}{4}$
- Square piece of paper

Explore
Ask each child to place the 4 whole objects in front of them.

Instructions (teacher to students)
1. One of the slices of bread will remain a *whole* one. Place the card showing 1 underneath this slice of bread.
2. Cut the next slice of bread in half. Place the $\frac{1}{2}$ card under these pieces of bread.
3. Cut the next slice of bread into thirds. Place the $\frac{1}{3}$ card under these pieces of bread.
4. The last slice of bread will be cut into quarters. Place the $\frac{1}{4}$ card under these pieces of bread.
5. What do you notice when you compare the denominator with the number of slices of bread you have cut each whole slice into?
6. Show me 2 halves of bread. We can write this as: $\frac{2}{2} = 1$.
7. Show me 2 thirds of bread. We write this as: $\frac{2}{3}$.
8. Show me 2 quarters of bread. We write this as: $\frac{2}{4} = \frac{1}{2}$
9. Following this pattern, see if you can work out how many thirds would make a whole 1 and how many quarters would make a whole 1.
10. Following the patterns we have looked at, see if you can work out how you would write: one third, three quarters, two thirds, four quarters as a number.
11. With this square piece of paper, show me two different ways we can split it into quarters.

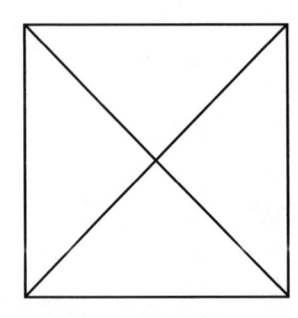

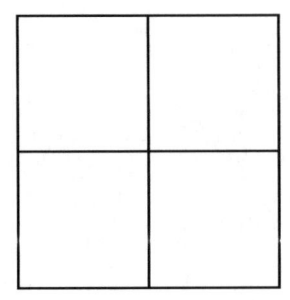

Explain
Explain to a partner why $\frac{4}{4}$, $\frac{3}{3}$ and $\frac{2}{2}$ each equals 1.

Activities

Adding fractions

Resources (per child)
- A set of magnetic fractions
- A mini whiteboard

Explore

Ask each child to explore the magnetic fractions by placing parts together to make whole numbers.

Instructions (teacher to students)

1. Show me $\frac{1}{4}$. If we add another $\frac{1}{4}$ to it, how many quarters do we have? We would write that as: $\frac{2}{4}$.

2. Show me $\frac{1}{6}$. If we add another $\frac{1}{6}$ to it, how many sixths do we have? We would write that as: $\frac{2}{6}$.

3. How do you think we would write three quarters as a number? Show me three quarters with your magnetic fractions.

4. How do you think we would write three sixths as a number? Show me three sixths with your magnetic fractions.

5. If we add $\frac{1}{6} + \frac{2}{6} = \frac{3}{6}$, what do you notice about the top number (numerator) and the bottom number (denominator)?

6. Add these together with your magnetic fractions, and then write them as sums:

   $\frac{1}{3} + \frac{1}{3} =$ _____

   $\frac{2}{6} + \frac{3}{6} =$ _____

   $\frac{1}{5} + \frac{2}{5} =$ _____

7. Place the fractions in order from smallest to largest, using your magnetic fractions. What do you notice?

   $\frac{1}{6} \quad \frac{1}{5} \quad \frac{1}{4} \quad \frac{1}{3} \quad \frac{1}{2}$

Explain

Explain to a partner how you add fractions together. Then explain why when the bottom number gets bigger (such as $\frac{1}{10}$ compared with $\frac{1}{5}$), the piece of the whole gets smaller.

Activities

Introducing decimals

Resources (per child)

- A set of play money
- Copy of the money chart, which differentiates whole numbers from part numbers (see below)

Explore

Ask each child to explore how many 10c, 20c and 50c make a dollar.

Instructions (teacher to students)

1. We are going to name the $1 coin the *whole* one. Anything less than a whole number is *part* of a dollar. Count out ten 10 cent pieces. How much money do we have altogether? Split those ten 10 cent pieces into 2 even piles. How many coins are in each pile? (5) From here, how can we work out how many cents are in half a dollar?

2. Let's place those five 10 cent pieces on the chart. We would call that $0.50

3. Let's place six 10 cent pieces on the chart. We would call that $0.60.

4. Try placing different amounts of 10 cents on the chart. How would you write it with a decimal point? What happens if you were to put ten 10 cent pieces on the chart? (It would make a dollar.) So which column would the dollar go in?

Money chart

$10	$1	10 cents

Explain

Explain to a partner why we write 70 cents as a decimal like this: $0.70.

© Essential Resources Educational Publishers Ltd, 2012

Activities

Shopping with money

Resources

- A set of play money
- Copy of the money chart, which differentiates whole numbers from part numbers (see page 31)
- An area that is set up as a shop, including with empty packets representing stock for sale

Explore

Label the packaging (cereal boxes, tins, pencils etc) with realistic prices. Research if necessary. Write the amounts correctly.

Instructions (teacher to students)

1. Four children will work in the shop at a time. Two people will "shop" and two people will be the "shopkeepers".

2. Let's all practise giving change. Have the money in front of you. If something costs $1.60 and I give the shopkeeper $2, how will I work out how much change to give?

   – I can add from 60 cents up to the next dollar: 70c, 80c, 90c, $1

   OR

   – I can say: 60 + ? = 100 ($1). The answer will be 40 cents

   OR

   – I can say: 50 + 50 = 100 ($1). If I add 10 cents to one side to make it up to 60 cents, I need to take off 10 cents on the other side so I will give 40 cents change.

3. When you give or receive change, try to think how you worked out *how* much change to give or how much you would get. Always check the correct change has been given.

Explain

Explain to a partner why knowing your addition facts to 10 (8 + 2, 7 + 3, 6 + 4, 5 + 5) is useful for when you are giving change up to a $1 (giving 80c for spending 20c, 70c for 30c, etc).

Activities

Decimal charts

Resources (per child)
- A copy of the decimal chart (see below)
- Pen or pencil

Explore
Ask each child to think about what a number would be called if it is in a specific column.

Instructions (teacher to students)

1. In your chart can you write the following:
   - 0.1
   - 0.23
   - 0.34
   - 2.34
   - 34.45
   - 41.2
   - 3.59

2. Now let's write them as fractions:
   - $\frac{1}{10}$
   - $\frac{23}{100}$
   - $\frac{34}{100}$
   - $2\frac{34}{100}$
   - $34\frac{45}{100}$
   - $41\frac{2}{10}$
   - $3\frac{59}{100}$

Explain
Explain to a partner why 0.34 is the same as $\frac{34}{100}$.

Decimal chart

Hundreds	Tens	Ones	.	Tenths	Hundredths

© Essential Resources Educational Publishers Ltd, 2012

Activities

Adding and subtracting decimals

Resources (per child)

- A copy of the decimal chart (see page 33)
- A set of magnetic decimal and fraction pieces
- Workbook and pen/pencil

Explore

- Ask each child to find 0.1 as a decimal magnetic piece. What would 0.2 look like?
- Ask each child to find 0.5 as a decimal magnetic piece. What would be the answer to:
  0.5 + 0.5 = __?

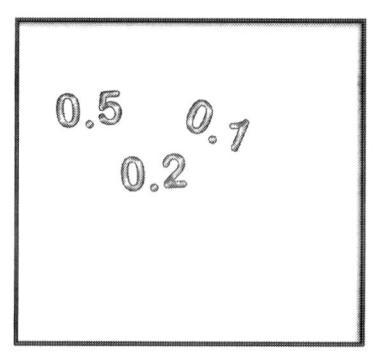

```
0.5   0.1
   0.2
```

Instructions (teacher to students)

1. Find 0.5 and 0.1. If we add them together it will look like this: 0.5 + 0.1 = 0.6. What do you notice when we add decimals together?
2. Let's add 0.4 + 0.2 = 0.6. What do you notice when we add these decimals together?
3. Complete these sums:

   0.2 + 0.3 =
   0.5 + 0.2 =
   0.6 + 0.1 =
   0.3 + 0.3 =

4. Now complete these sums:

   0.6 + 0.4 =
   0.7 + 0.3 =
   0.8 + 0.2 =
   0.9 + 0.1 =

Explain

Explain to a partner why 0.6 + 0.4 = 1.

> Activities

Subtracting using equal addition

Resources (per child)
- 40 blocks
- Piece of A4 size cloth

Explore

Ask each child to explore *difference* between numbers (revisiting the concept from the activity "Subtracting can show difference", page 21).

- Place 5 on one side and 7 on the other side of the cloth. What is the difference between the two numbers? (2)
- If we add 3 to the 5 (so it now becomes 8) and we add 3 to the 7 (so it now becomes 10), what is the difference between the two numbers now? (It is still 2.)
- This means if I *add* the same number to each number in a subtraction equation the *difference* will remain the same.

Instructions (teacher to students)

1. On one side of the cloth, place a line of 19 blocks. On the other side of the cloth, place a line of 7 blocks. 19 subtract 7 is the same as the *difference* between these two numbers. Let's add *1* to 19 (to make it easier to work with) and let's add *1* to 7.

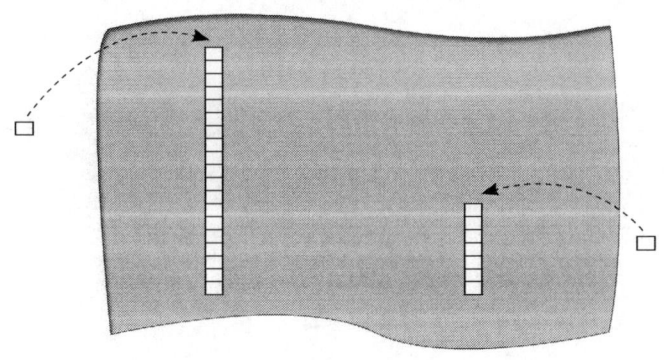

    - We had 19 – 7.
    - Now we have 20 – 8.
    - The answer is 12.

2. We will subtract these together using the *equal addition* strategy:
    - 18 – 9 = __ Let's add 2 to each number, to make it: 20 – 11 =
    - 17 – 9 =
    - 28 – 9 =
    - 37 – 9 =
    - 49 – 8 =

Explain

Explain to a partner why we can use the *equal addition* strategy when subtracting. The key word is *difference* (between two numbers).

Activities

Groups of tables

Resources (per child)

- 30 blocks
- Workbook
- Coloured pencils

Explore

Ask each child to place blocks into groups of three. What do 4 groups of 3 look like? What do 7 groups of 3 look like?

Instructions (teacher to students)

1. Write this chart in your book with a different colour for each line:

   3   1 × 3 = 3
   3 3   2 × 3 = 6 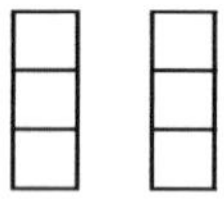
   3 3 3   3 × 3 = 9
   3 3 3 3   4 × 3 = 12
   3 3 3 3 3   5 × 3 = 15 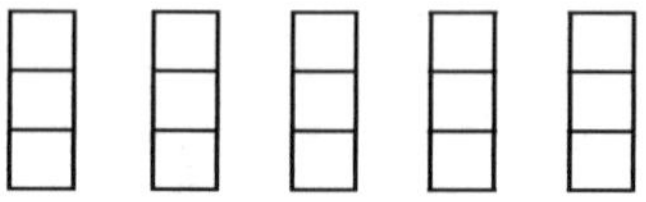
   3 3 3 3 3 3   6 × 3 = 18
   3 3 3 3 3 3 3   7 × 3 = 21
   3 3 3 3 3 3 3 3   8 × 3 = 24 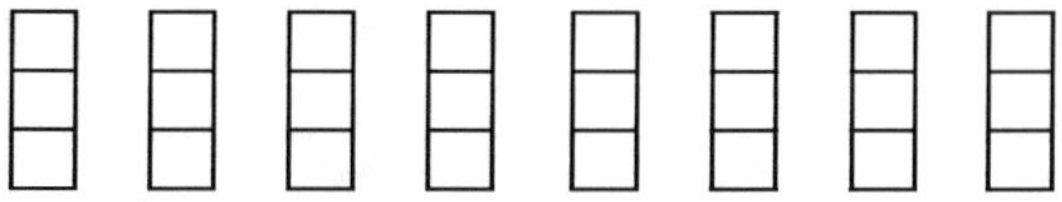
   3 3 3 3 3 3 3 3 3   9 × 3 = 27
   3 3 3 3 3 3 3 3 3 3   10 × 3 = 30

2. Find the line that has 5 lots of 3. What is 5 lots of 3 altogether?
3. Find the line that has 7 lots of 3. What is 7 lots of 3 altogether?
4. Find the line that has 3 lots of 3. What is 3 lots of 3 altogether?
5. Find the line that has 6 lots of 3. What is 6 lots of 3 altogether?
6. Find the line that has 9 lots of 3. What is 9 lots of 3 altogether?
7. What are the two ways I can write 8 lots of 3?
8. What are the two ways I can write 10 lots of 3?

Explain

Explain to a partner why there are two ways to write 4 lots of 3. Explain to a friend which is the quickest way to write 4 lots of 3.

> Activities

Sharing groups of tables

Resources (per child)

- 30 blocks
- Workbook containing the "groups of 3" chart (see page 36)

Explore

Ask each child to place 18 blocks in front of them. If they share the 18 blocks equally between 6 people, how many blocks will each person get? How does this connect to making 6 groups of 3?

Instructions (teacher to students)

1. Find the chart in your workbook that shows groups of 3.

2. Place 12 blocks in front of you. Share these 12 blocks between 4 people. How many blocks will each person get? Now share the 12 blocks between 3 people. How many blocks will each person get?

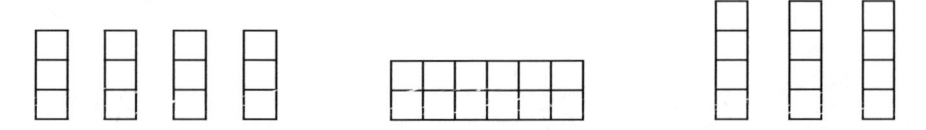

3. Place 15 blocks in front of you. Share these 15 blocks between 5 people. How many blocks will each person get? Now share the 15 blocks between 3 people. How many blocks will each person get?

4. Place 21 blocks in front of you. Share these 21 blocks between 7 people. How many blocks will each person get? Now share the 21 blocks between 3 people. How many blocks will each person get?

5. What patterns and connections are you beginning to see between grouping numbers in lots of 3 and sharing numbers in this pattern?

6. Explain to a partner why 9 groups of 3 is 27 and 3 groups of 9 is 27. Show your partner this using blocks. Now let your partner show you why the *answer* (27) can be shared between 9 people and also shared between 3 people. Finally swap over so that you both explain the point that the other person did last time.

7. Using a diagram show: $10 \times 3 = 30$; $3 \times 10 = 30$; 30 shared between 10 is 3; and 30 shared between 3 is 10.

8. Using a diagram show: $2 \times 3 = 6$; $3 \times 2 = 6$; 6 shared between 2 is 3; and 6 shared between 3 is 2.

Explain

Explain to a partner the family of facts for multiplying and dividing. Choose a particular sum that you have used, for example $4 \times 3 = 12$, and demonstrate your thinking using blocks or a diagram. Use words to explain as well.

© Essential Resources Educational Publishers Ltd, 2012

Times tables

Thinking about times tables for children with dyscalculia

Two essential areas for learning the times tables – number sense and long-term memory – are, unfortunately, weak in a child with dyscalculia. As a consequence, learning the times tables can be a painful experience for the child – and the adult! This section offers some key ideas as well as a programme of work to help both the child and the teacher be more productive during their time spent on the times tables.

Important points

1. To learn their times tables, a child with dyscalculia will need *lots* of repetition. Make the repetition more fun by constantly finding new ways to practise, such as saying the times tables while throwing and catching a ball, jumping on a rebounder or playing hopscotch-type games.

2. For each times table, introduce the concrete learning first and then work on learning the answers.

3. Make sure children connect the answer to the question. Some children learn to count up in threes or fours but do not know which answer connects to which question.

4. Set the child to learn their tables in *order* before learning them out of order. The child may need to work on the times table in order for a lot longer than you might imagine.

5. Only move on to a new times table once a child is very confident with the times table they have been focusing on. The child will need their times tables for life – what are a few extra months (years) spent on them if they learn them well?

6. Give the child lots of clear visuals. For example, if they are learning the 4 times table, only display the 4 times table on the wall.

7. Use lots of multisensory ideas (music, visuals, moving etc) so that if there is a blank with one strategy, another strategy may work.

8. When you introduce a new times table, keep revising the previous times table.

9. Practise *every* day.

10. Break each times table into colour-coded sections for the child to learn one section at a time.

Times tables

2 times table

Resources

- Cubes that interlock
- Magnetic counters
- Small pieces of paper (business card size)
- Pens

Explore

Ask each child to create pairs of interlocking cubes and pairs of magnetic counters. Do they notice any patterns? (For example, 2 groups of 2 is 4 – the same as 2 + 2; all the twos when added up create even numbers – why is this?)

Instructions (teacher to students)

1. Make 3 sets of 2 by connecting the cubes in pairs. How many cubes do we have all together? Another way to write this is: 3 × 2 = 6.

2. The × sign means "groups of". Let's try with these ones:
   - Make 4 groups of 2. How many do we have altogether?
     Make 5 groups of 2. How many do we have altogether?
   - This is how we write those sums: 4 × 2 = 8; 5 × 2 = 10.

3. With your cubes, make groups of 2, up to 10 groups of 2. You are going to make 1 group of 2, then 2 groups of 2, then 3 groups of 2 and so on. Place the groups in ascending order.

4. Write each of these numbers on a separate piece of paper: 2, 4, 6, 8, 10, 12, 14, 16, 18, 20. Place each piece of paper in front of the appropriate group of 2.

5. Let's look at 10. How many groups of 2 are next to the number 10? (5) That means we can write: 5 × 2 = 10. If × means "groups of", it also means I can write: 5 + 5 = 10.

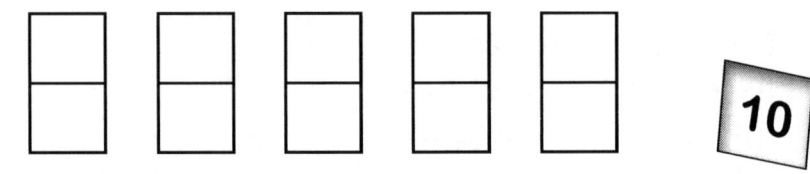

6. Let's look at 12. How many groups of 2 are next to the number 12? (6) That means we can write: 6 × 2 = 12 and 6 + 6 = 12.

7. (Repeat the process in steps 5–6 slowly with all the answers in the 2 times table.)

Explain

Explain to your partner how we can write the sum for each lot of "groups of 2" we have. See if you can write the sum both ways: by multiplying and by adding.

Times tables

Dividing with the 2 times table

Resources
- A copy of the 2 times table
- Connecting blocks or cubes

Explore
Ask each child to connect and split groups of blocks.

Instructions (teacher to students)

1. Make 3 sets of 2. How many cubes do we have altogether? (6) Let's write: $3 \times 2 = 6$.

2. Put 6 blocks together. Share these 6 blocks equally between 3 people. How many blocks will they get each? (2) What do you notice when you compare $3 \times 2 = 6$ and $6 \div 3 = 2$? Let's unpack this pattern and see why it happens. (Respond to the children's discoveries appropriately.)

3. Make 4 sets of 2. How many cubes do we have altogether? (8) Let's write: $4 \times 2 = 8$.

4. Put 8 blocks together. Share these 8 blocks equally between 4 people. How many blocks will they get each? What do you notice when you compare $4 \times 2 = 8$ and $8 \div 4 = 2$? Let's unlock this pattern and see why it happens.

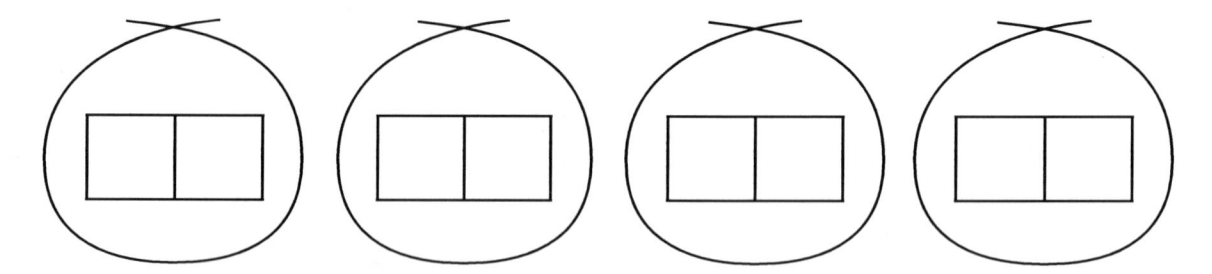

5. (Repeat the process in steps 2–4 until children are responding with lots of "I get it now" and "I can see it now". Ask the children to tell and explain the patterns they notice.)

6. I am going to answer the sum: $6 \div 3 = \_\_$ To answer this sum I am going to think, in my head, the opposite of division – multiplying; I am going to think: $3 \times 2 = 6$. Therefore $6 \div 3$ must be 2. Let's do this with our blocks to check. Are we correct?

7. (Repeat the process in step 6 for all the 2 times table.)

Next steps
When you are sure that all the children understand the concept of multiplying and dividing within their 2 times table, practise different ways to remember the facts. For example, the children do star jumps while answering the 2 times table, changing the direction they are facing after every four answers; jump the answers on a rebounder; and/or test each other.

Explain
Explain to your partner the relationship between multiplying and dividing.

Times tables

3 times table

Resources

- A 3 times table chart that is colour coordinated, for example:
    - purple: 1 × 3, 2 × 3, 3 × 3
    - green: 4 × 3, 5 × 3, 6 × 3
    - black: 7 × 3, 8 × 3, 9 × 3
    - blue: 10 × 3, 11 × 3, 12 × 3

  or another colour combination of your choice

- Pieces of A5 paper
- Coloured felt pens or pencils, matching the colours on the chart
- Ball per child

Explore

Ask each child say the answers to the 3 times table while looking at the chart. What patterns do they notice?

Instructions (teacher to students)

1. Using a purple felt pen, write each of these numbers on a separate piece of paper: 3, 6, 9. Place the pieces of paper on the floor in front of you. When I say a sum, throw the ball on the answer and call the answer out: 1 × 3 = __ ; 2 × 3 = __ ; 3 × 3 = __

   > 2 x 3 = | 3 | 6 | 9 |

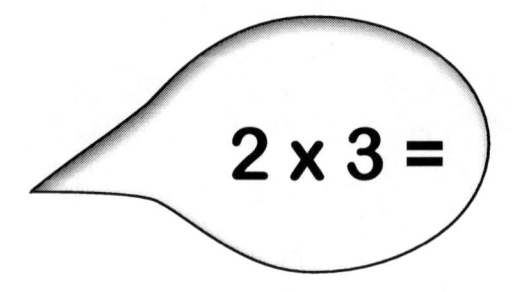

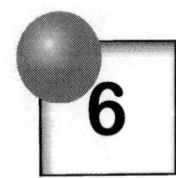

2. Using a green felt pen, write each of these numbers on a separate piece of paper: 12, 15, 18. Place the pieces of paper on the floor in front of you, next to the other numbers. When I say a sum, throw the ball on the answer and call out the answer.

3. (Repeat the process in steps 1–2 for the next two sets of answers for the 3 times table.)

4. Which coloured section is the trickiest for you to remember the answers to? Whichever section it is, practise that section and create a different activity with the ball, or without the ball, to help you remember the answers.

Explain

Explain to your partner which is the easiest section of the 3 times table for you to learn, and which is the trickiest. Explain and demonstrate to your partner how you are going to remember the answers to your trickiest part of the 3 times table.

© Essential Resources Educational Publishers Ltd, 2012

Times tables

Dividing with the 3 times table

Resources

- A copy of the 3 times table, colour coordinated (see page 41 for suggested colour combination)
- Connecting blocks or cubes

Explore

Ask each child to connect and split groups of 3 blocks. How many groups do we need to make: 12, 15, 18?

Instructions (teacher to students)

1. With the cubes, make 6 groups of 3. How many do we have altogether? Find the sum on the chart. If we have 18 blocks and divide them between 6 people, how many will each person have? Write this as a sum and show this with your blocks.

2. With the cubes, make 7 groups of 3. How many do we have altogether? Find the sum on the chart. If we have 21 blocks and divide them between 7 people, how many will each person have? If we have 21 blocks and divide them between 3 people, how many will each person have? Write these as sums and show with your blocks.

3. (Repeat the process in step 2 with all of the 3 times table, looking at the connection between multiplying and dividing.)

$$4 \times 3 = 12 \quad 1 + 2 = 3$$
$$5 \times 3 = 15 \quad 1 + 5 = 6$$
$$6 \times 3 = 18 \quad 1 + 8 = 9$$

4. Let's look at the patterns in the answers to the 3 times table. The answers go odd, even, odd, even: 3, 6, 9, 12, 15, 18 and so on. All the answers can be added to either 3, 6 or 9.

5. Without looking at the chart, let's think about what is: 4×3? So if it is 12, what is 12 shared equally between 3?

Next steps

When you are sure that all the children understand the concept of multiplying and dividing within their 3 times table, practise different ways to remember the facts. For example, children do star jumps while answering the 3 times table; and/or you call out for the answers to *purple* sums, *green* sums etc.

Explain

Explain to your partner how and why 18 shared between 3 is 6, and 18 shared between 6 is 3.

Times tables

4 times table

Resources

- A 4 times table chart, colour coordinated, for example:
    - purple: 1 × 4, 2 × 4, 3 × 4
    - green: 4 × 4, 5 × 4, 6 × 4
    - black: 7 × 4, 8 × 4, 9 × 4
    - blue: 10 × 4, 11 × 4, 12 × 4

  or another colour combination of your choice

- Small square pieces of paper
- Pens
- Bean bags
- Workbooks

Explore

Ask each child to say the answers to the times table while looking at the chart. What patterns do they notice? Do they notice that all the answers in the 4 times table are even numbers?

Instructions (teacher to students)

1. Write each answer in the 4 times table on a separate piece of paper: 4, 8, 12, 16, 20, 24, 28, 32, 36, 40, 44, 48. Place them in a circle on the floor. As I call out the sum, stand on or next to the answer: 1 × 4 = __; 2 × 4 = __ etc.

2. Turn two of the numbers face down. We will go around the circle and you will say the answers to all of the 4 times table, including the answers that are hidden from you. You will need to remember each answer you can't see.

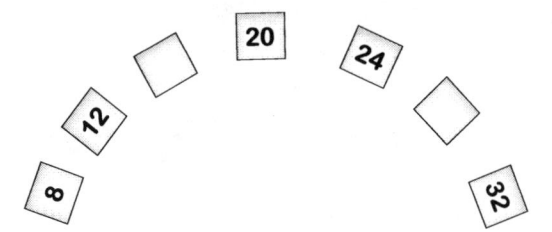

3. Turn over another two pieces of paper so now you have four hidden answers. We will go around the circle again, with everyone saying the answers to all of the 4 times table.

4. See how many pieces of paper you feel confident about turning face down (so you can't see the answer). Give the answers to the 4 times table.

5. Turn the pieces of paper face up so you can see all of the answers. This time I will say the 4 times table sums out of order (4 × 4, 6 × 4, 2 × 4 etc). Throw a bean bag on the correct answer.

6. Let's write our 4 times table down in our book.

Explain

Explain to your partner how we know all the answers in the 4 times table are even numbers.

Times tables

Dividing with the 4 times table

Resources

- A copy of the 4 times table, colour coordinated (see page 43 for suggested colour combination)
- Play money

Explore

Ask each child to count, sort and order the money.

Instructions (teacher to students)

1. Sort the money into groups of coins that are worth the same amount. Choose one type of coin: these are the coins you will use for this activity.
2. Find another person who has the same type of coins as you. Put your coins together. You need at least 40 coins.
3. Share 40 coins between 4 people. How many coins does each person get?
4. Share 36 coins between 4 people. How many coins does each person get?
5. Share 32 coins between 4 people. How many coins does each person get?
6. (Repeat the process in steps 3–5 for all of the answers in the 4 times table.)
7. Create five stories using sharing/division and the 4 times table. Here are some examples:
   - Show me this story: There was a king who had 16 gold coins. He had 4 sons and wanted to share the coins equally. Each son received 4 coins.
   - Show me this story: There was a wizard who had 20 gold cauldrons. He had to share them between his 5 training wizards. They each got 4 cauldrons.
   - Show me this story: There were 6 miners who found 24 pieces of gold in the mines. They shared the gold and each miner took 4 pieces of gold home

Next steps

Make a book with all the stories involving sharing with the 4 times table (and for each other times table as well if you wish).

Explain

Explain to your partner how and why each answer in the 4 times table (eg, 16 is the answer to 4 × 4) is the same as the quantity we start with when using a related dividing sum (eg, 16 ÷ 4 = 4).

Times tables

5 times table

Resources

- A 5 times table chart, colour coordinated, for example:
  - purple: 1 × 5, 2 × 5, 3 × 5
  - green: 4 × 5, 5 × 5, 6 × 5
  - black: 7 × 5, 8 × 5, 9 × 5
  - blue: 10 × 5, 11 × 5, 12 × 5

  or another colour combination of your choice
- Small square pieces of paper
- Pens

Explore

Ask each child to look at how each answer in the 5 times table has either 5 or 0 as the last number.

Instructions (teacher to students)

1. Write each answer to the 5 times table on a separate piece of paper.

2. Place the answers that have a 5 as the last number in a line on one side, and the answers that have a 0 as the last number on the other side, like this:

5	10
15	20
25	30
35	40

3. With one foot, stand on the 5, then with your other foot stand on the 10. Go from side to side, saying the numbers up to 50 (10 × 5).

4. (Repeat step 3 but this time the children go backwards from 50.)

5. (Repeat step 4, but this time without the numbers on the floor or with some turned face down.)

Explain

Explain to your partner how we know that all the answers in the 5 times table end in either 5 or 0.

© Essential Resources Educational Publishers Ltd, 2012

Times tables

Dividing with the 5 times table

Resources

- A copy of the 5 times table, colour coordinated (see page 45 for suggested colour combination)
- Glass crystals

Explore

Ask each child to count the glass crystals into groups of 5.

Instructions

1. Show me 2 groups of 5 crystals. How many do we have altogether?

2. Show me 3 groups of 5 crystals. How many do we have altogether?
3. Show me 4 groups of 5 crystals. How many do we have altogether?
4. Show me 5 groups of 5 crystals. How many do we have altogether?
5. What is the pattern when we have an *even* number of groups? (The answer ends in a 0.) When we have an *odd* number of groups, the answer ends in a …?
6. Let's call out in fives up to 100. Let's see if we can do that backwards as well.

$$25 \div 5 = 5$$

7. Show me 5 groups of crystals. I have 25 altogether. If we share these crystals between 5 people, how many will each person have? Show me that as a division sum.
8. (Repeat the process in step 7 with other answers in the 5 times table.)

Explain

Explain to a partner why, if the first number in your sum is an *even* number in the 5 times table, then you know that when you divide it the answer will be an even number. For example, $20 \div 5 = 4$; $30 \div 5 = 6$; $40 \div 5 = 8$. (Obviously if we divide the other way, $40 \div 8$, our answer will be 5, which is an odd number.)

General times table games

The next times tables (6–10) can follow the pattern of teaching set out in the 2–5 times tables above, adapted to each specific times table. Below is a variety of other games that can be used for all the times tables.

- **Bean bag circle**: Sitting in a circle, children pass around a bean bag. When it is their turn for the bean bag, a child says the answer to a times table sum.

- **Grab the tail**: On long strips of paper, write the answers to one of the times tables. Hand them out to the children, who hang the strips out of a back pocket or over a waistband like a tail. Each person tries to grab as many "tails" from other children as possible. Once all the tails have been claimed, each child has to write the sum to connect to the correct answer on each tail in their possession. One point is scored for each correct sum matching to a tail.

- **Charades**: In pairs, children stand up in front of a group and have a sum and an answer (for example: 4 × 3 = 12). They have to act out the sum in any way possible except by talking, pointing to numbers or holding up fingers. Some options are to:
  - point to their ear for "sounds like" then to a door because the first number in the sum, 4, sounds like *door*
  - stamp their feet – three stamps for the number 3
  - move – twelve press-ups means 12 (each child in the pair might do six).

- **It's me**: Give each child a number that is the answer to a sum in a given times table. For example, for the 6 times table you might give one child the number 18, another child 42 and so on. One child calls out times table sums, such as: 3 × 6. The person who has the answer stands up. The idea is to go quite fast. If the group is large, more than one person can have the same answer – then it is a race to see who stands up first and at the correct time. Answers can be swapped around.

© Essential Resources Educational Publishers Ltd, 2012

Maths activities

These activities offer children who struggle with maths opportunities to practise concepts in a relaxed way. They are also suitable for all other children in the class. They are useful for those times (which are very rare these days for teacher and students) when the testing is over and the curriculum pressure has eased.

Shop

Set up a shop in the class. The shop can be real (such as for a fundraising activity, selling popcorn, drinks or other snacks) or "pretend" with boxes, objects and toys the children have set up. Very young children are often allowed to set up a shop in their learning space – but many older children love this activity too.

Sorting

Bring in objects – buttons, glass stones, pebbles, shells – for the children to count and organise into boxes or bags.

Maths volleyball

Set up a volleyball net. Children have to pass the ball back and forth counting in twos, threes, fives or whatever concept is the focus of the maths lesson.

Movement times tables

In groups, the children create a movement sequence that they do while chanting their times tables. Music can be used. Possible movements include star jumps, marching, jumping forward and backward, turning squats, and leaps.

Lolly jars

Fill lolly jars with lollies, but also buttons, stones, shells, counters. See who can estimate the number in the jar.

Treasure hunt

Write the answers to at least four different times tables on pieces of card – one answer per card. Place the cards around the room. Arrange the children into four groups (or more if you have displayed more than four different times tables) and allocate a times table to each group.

Each group walks around the room looking for the answers to their times table. They are allowed to pick up 12 answers. The first group to pick up the correct answers to their times table is the winner. If a group has picked up an incorrect answer (for example, if the 4 times table group picks up 15), they have to negotiate with another group to get the correct answer. (There may be more than two groups negotiating to get the answers they need.)

Maths activities

Play dough

Organise children into groups and allocate a times table to each group. Each group creates groups of objects for their times table. For example, the 3 times table group may create candles and place them in groups of three. If each cake has three candles, how many play dough cakes will we need?

Other ideas for objects to create from play dough are: sausages (how many plates required), biscuits (how many plates required), skittles (how many balls required) and fish (how many ponds required).

Note: If play dough raises cultural concerns in your school due to its food ingredients, it may be appropriate to substitute another material such as clay or plasticine.

Home run

In pairs, children find a space they label *Home*. Between their Home and the mat area, each pair places 10 cut-out feet along the floor as the steps they need to take to get Home from the mat.

Call out a number, such as 23. The first pair to come up with a number story for that number (eg, 15 eggs plus 8 eggs = 23 eggs) can take one step towards home. The first pair home wins.

Under my chair

This can be run as a whole-class activity or, if it is a big class, in groups.

The children sit in a circle with a chair in the centre. One child chooses a number between 1 and 20 (or 20 and 40), writes this number on a card and places it under the chair (face down). The rest of the children take turns to give a sum, such as 7 × 2 or 10 – 6. If the answer to the sum is the same as the number under the chair, the child who called it out gets the number and it is their turn to create a number for under the chair.

You can allow children to suggest all types of sums or limit them to, for example, subtraction or multiplication only.

Fizz buzz

Sitting in a circle, children take turns to say one sum in the five times table, going in order through the table. Whenever they get to an answer that contains 5, the child says *fizz* is said instead of the number. On the second round, they say *buzz* instead of any answers containing 10.

© Essential Resources Educational Publishers Ltd, 2012

Assessment

In this final section we look at assessment for children with dyscalculia. We consider effective approaches with these children to assess both maths strategies and knowledge generally and dyscalculia and maths difficulties specifically.

Assessment for general maths knowledge and strategies

There are many excellent assessment tools for maths in general at the primary school level. Many of these assessments check knowledge and strategies for answering sums and problems. However, for the child with real maths difficulties some processes can slip through the net. You need to be extra diligent and aware that children who struggle in maths will often find innovative ways to cover up their difficulties. Some of the common ways are to:

- call out an answer a split second after another person has called out the answer

- check their work with a friend who is good at maths and change their own answers
- stay extra quiet if the teacher is looking for someone to answer a question.

However, also remember that for the child who struggles at maths it is excruciatingly nerve-racking to have to call out an answer in the class (and very embarrassing if the answer is incorrect). In addition, this child will be highly nervous when being assessed on a one-to-one basis and may assess even lower because of this nervousness.

When you are assessing knowledge (such as basic facts to 10), the child who struggles with maths may initially not know the answers (or only if they use their fingers). On a further assessment the child may still score poorly at the same basic facts; however, they may have actually made progress by moving from making no connection for "3 + 4 = 7, therefore 3 + 5 = 8" to making a connection and seeing why this happens mathematically. This is a significant movement forward for the child with dyscalculia but will not necessarily show up on a knowledge test (or even a strategy test). For this reason it is often best to "assess" a child who struggles with maths by working one-to-one with them and observing how they attempt to solve problems.

Concept before speed

Children who struggle with maths will need to feel very confident in any area before they can be assessed to complete specific facts in a given time. Indeed many children with dyscalculia will always struggle with coming up with the answers as quickly as their peers. If the child understands the concept (eg, that 3 + 7 = 10 and if 1 is moved from the 3 to the 7 it will make 2 + 8 = 10), the most useful approach could be to move the child to the next stage and accept they will not succeed in a "speed test". If you keep a child at the same level for a long period due to their inability to answer quickly, this child may switch off and become bored and disheartened with maths.

> Assessment

Understanding the question

When assessing a child with dyscalculia, do check that the child really understands what you are asking of them. Often children will think they are being asked something much more difficult than they really are.

Assessment for dyscalculia and maths difficulties

The criteria set out on the assessment sheet below are indicators that maths is difficult for a child. This assessment is relevant to any child aged six years or older at primary school who is not progressing as expected in maths. Its purpose is to give a quick indicator of a child's abilities and difficulties. If a child meets more than six of the indicators, a thorough assessment may be required.

Where a child meets several of these indicators, they will need extra support in the form of hands-on resources, time, repetition and revision of basic maths knowledge.

Note: Several issues may affect maths learning such as ADHD (tricky to concentrate), dyslexia (weak memory, cannot read the questions) and dyspraxia (clumsy use of resources). However, in the end the child who struggles with maths for whatever reason will need the support and multisensory style of teaching set out in this series.

Quick indicator assessment for maths difficulties

Name of child:	
Anxiety levels	
Finds it hard to settle in the maths class (fidgeting, going to the toilet, sharpening pencil etc).	☐
Only answers if specifically asked a question.	☐
Waits for other children to answer.	☐
Speaks the answer quietly.	☐
Number sense	
Counts on fingers and then checks the counting by counting on fingers again.	☐
Is not sure of answer unless can check on fingers.	☐
Counts 1–1 inaccurately, either with fingers or resources.	☐
Does not notice inaccuracy (eg, says it is 11 when only has 10 counters).	☐
Always counts from the beginning if given a sum (eg, 5 + 3 – will count the 5 out and then the 3).	☐
Memory	
Does not remember facts from one week to the next.	☐
Does not make connections with previous learning/lesson.	☐
Does not move on from 1–1 counting or does so very reluctantly.	☐
Progress is extremely slow.	☐

© Essential Resources Educational Publishers Ltd, 2012

Assessment

One-on-one observation

The chart on page 54 offers a gentle series of activities to find out how a child "sees" maths and their level of number sense. You might choose to work through them in one session or in several mini sessions. Questions can be adapted as appropriate for each child.

Critical to an effective assessment is to prepare the child sufficiently for it. Below are guidelines for familiarising the child with the language of assessment and providing them with plenty of opportunities for practice. Thereafter the guidelines for observation are designed to help you conduct your observation. You may find it helpful to refer to them in completing the "Notes" column in the activities sheet.

Guidelines for assisting with language

Where a child struggles with and is anxious about maths and then has an assessment, they are working from their *worst* possible ability. Moreover, given that written and one-to-one assessments can use slightly different language from that used in the everyday mathematics lessons, a child can be really thrown off kilter in this situation.

To minimise the issues, practise the language prior to assessments:

- Unpack assessment language for a child *before* the assessment and before the anxiety sets in.

- The language of assessments can be very formal. Let the child *hear* how the questions may be asked or written.

- Check the child understands specific language.

    Example
    What does before mean? Can you show me?

- Check the child understands language that has the same meaning.

    Example
    Do you know that *groups of*, *lots of* and *multiply* all mean the same thing?

- Explicitly explain to the child what is expected.

    Example
    When I ask this …. I will be looking for this …

- Give a child examples of how you work through relevant problems.

    Example
    Explain how you did the workings for this sum.

- Give the child the opportunity to become comfortable and familiar with the language of assessments.

Assessment

Opportunities for practice: think outside the box

It often throws me off guard when I notice the way in which some children get in a muddle with mathematics. For example, some children get confused by the number that indicates the number or order of the sums in a given test. They mix this number into the sum and get quite confused. Other children miss out a number in the sequence of questions, which means that for the rest of the test they are out of sequence and consequently get their answers incorrect. These seemingly simple mistakes can have dire consequences for all children – but especially for the child who already struggles.

Secondary students have lots of practice revising for exams, in all subjects. They work on past tests and become comfortable with the type of questions they will be asked. This kind of process needs to happen at primary school for children with dyscalculia too.

Guidelines for observation

Look for the following as you work through the assessment activities with the child.

- Facial expressions: Does the child look puzzled, worried, confused?
- Does the child have to keep checking with you about what you mean?
- Does the child have to repeat the question or ask for the question to be repeated before they can start?
- Does the child have to count every block to check?
- How quickly and confidently does the child answer the question?
- Is the child offering connections that are relevant to the mathematical patterns?
- Is the child offering connections that are relevant to the mathematical patterns even when not being asked to?
- If a child does not understand a concept, how far do you have to unpack the concept, and how many times do you have to do this before the child makes the connection (if they make the connection at all)?
- Can the child tell you what they see or what they have done?
- Does the child overlook "mistakes" or do they look puzzled? (For example, if they have accidentally counted out 11 blocks instead of 10 blocks for the tower block, then add 2 and get 13 altogether, do they just say, "It is 13" or do they say, "Something's not right"?)
- Are they systematic or disorganised in their work?
- Does the child get distracted easily?
- Does the child focus on connections that are not relevant to the question (such as choosing the colour of the blocks or thinking about the container for the blocks)?
- How does the child respond if they do not understand something?

Assessment

Activities for one-on-one observation

Activities	Notes
Ask the child to share 60 between 6 people (with counters or without). Ask the child to put 20 blocks in a system that makes them easier to count (tens or fives). How do they do this? Tell the child to show you 5 groups of 6. How do they do this? Ask, "What would be the quickest way to show 200 with the blocks?" Ask the child to circle all the multiples of 3 on a hundred square. What do they notice? Ask the child to circle all the multiples of 5 on a hundred square. What do they notice? Ask the child: • There were 50 birds. Then 3 flew away. How many are left? • There were 100 tigers at the zoo. Then 13 escaped. How many are left? Ask the child to answer the 3 times table as quickly as they can. Which, if any, questions do they get stuck on? Repeat with other targeted times tables. Ask the child: • There were 28 apples in the bucket. Now 5 more have been added. How many apples are there altogether? • There are 100 raffle tickets in one book and 55 raffle tickets in the second book. How many are there altogether? Ask, "How many tens in 110?" "How many fives in 50?" Ask the child to show you with the blocks: 104; 4 groups of 10; 3 groups of 6. Ask the child to place magnetic fractions in order from smallest to largest. Ask the child: • Which number comes after 99? • Which number comes before 89? • Write the number 111.	

Index of maths concepts

The activities in this book cover the following maths concepts.

adding	11–15, 17, 18, 23–25	number line	19
adding decimals	34	number stories	19, 22, 44, 49
adding fractions	30	odd numbers	11
adding in tens	11	partitioning	15–18, 23, 24
after	10	patterns	13, 22, 27
before	10	place value	15–24
counting back	13	quarters	29
counting on	12, 13	recognising 1–100	10, 11
decimals	31, 33, 34	re-grouping	23, 24
difference	21, 35	splitting numbers	16, 25
dividing	37, 40, 42, 44, 46	strategies	15–18, 23, 24, 26, 27, 32, 35
equal addition	35	subtracting	11–14, 19–22, 26, 35
even numbers	11	subtracting decimals	34
estimating	48	thirds	29
family of facts	14, 37	three dimensions	9
fractions	9, 27–30, 33	times tables	
"groups of"	39	two	39
groups of 10	26	three	9, 36, 37, 41
groups of tables	36, 37	four	43
halves	27–29	five	45, 49
hundred square	11–14	visualising	43
making sums	25	wholes	28, 29
money	9, 31, 32, 44	word problems	18, 23
multiplying	9, 36, 37, 39, 41, 43, 45, 47–49		

© Essential Resources Educational Publishers Ltd, 2012

CPSIA information can be obtained at www.ICGtesting.com
Printed in the USA
BVOC01s1130140916

461976BV00043B/111/P

9 781927 190845